Family from Ferrum

Priscilla Elliott

Printed in the United States of America

ISBN 979-8-218-90076-2 (paperback)

For my family, and for my children,
who carry what came before and what will follow.

Family from Ferrum

Characters

Johnathan

Black man, late twenties to early thirties. A millennial. Easily bothered and technology driven. From the South, but not Southern. Accustomed to information being accessible and unsettled when systems fail to provide clear answers.

Lisa

Black woman, early fifties. Southern belle. Runs the post office and is the self-proclaimed historian of Ferrum. Harold's younger sister and Junie Mae's daughter. Proud, measured, and protective of how the town's history is preserved and understood.

Harold

Black man, late fifties. Heavy Southern accent. Comfortable with himself and unfiltered. Has never left his hometown. Lisa's older brother and Melissa's father. Firmly rooted in tradition and routine.

Melissa

Black woman, twenties. A nonchalant millennial. A lesbian, against her father's hopes. Harold's daughter. Observant, restrained, and eager for a life beyond Ferrum.

Junie Mae

Black woman, seventies. Southern accent. Frail but strong willed. Holds the town's living memory in ways no record can.

Setting

Place

Ferrum, a small, old Southern town with a large majority Black population.

Time

Present day.

Environment

Ferrum has not been changed or updated for years. This stagnation is reflected in both the tone of the play and the people who live there. Routine governs daily life, and tradition is treated as protection rather than choice.

Locations

The first two acts move between a gas station convenience store and a post office, both located in the center of town. These public spaces serve as gathering points where history, conversation, and control intersect.

The third act takes place in Junie Mae's dining room, a private space where family, memory, and truth converge.

A table, chairs, and a bookshelf occupy the post office. Sitting at the table reading a book is Lisa.

Lisa finishes her book and puts it back on the shelf. She grabs a broom and starts sweeping the floor, humming a familiar tune.

A store bell rings. Johnathan enters stage left. Lisa doesn't look up from her sweeping because she's certain she knows who it is. She doesn't get many of visitors.

Lisa: You know Harold, I think I'm going to do something special for dinner at mama's this evening. Ain't you tired of the same last Friday meal each and every time. You know what? Tonight I'm making hibachi!

Johnathan: Ma'am?

(Lisa turns around startled.)

Lisa: Well then, you're not Harold at all. Hello young man, how can I help you?

Johnathan: Uh, hi. My name is Johnathan and I'm trying to find some information about someone who may have lived here. I did a search for the Ferrum history center on my Google Maps and it sent me to this location.

Lisa: Well I'm glad that Google works. Welcome!

Johnathan: But outside says the post office?

Lisa: Little town like ours doesn't need to have a separate building for both. Been that way since as long as I can remember, no need to fix what ain't broken honey. My name is Lisa Warner-Wilson.

(Lisa walks over to the bookshelf and showcases it with pride.)

Lisa: And here is our history center. Organized and maintained by yours truly.

(The store bell rings. Johnathan looks to the door. Beat. No one enters. He looks back to Lisa who didn't seem to notice the sound.)

Lisa: We don't get a lot of outsiders coming here too often. What is it that I can do for you?

Johnathan: Well ma'am, my name is Johnathan... Barnes the Third. I found this picture of who I believe to be my grandfather and written on the bottom corner was what I believe to be a location, Ferrum. A quick search online showed me that this is the only Ferrum in the south so here I am. You see my father didn't know much about his father. All he knew was that he was born in the south and moved up north to New York at some point because that's where he, meaning my father, was born. He, my grandfather, died when my father was a baby. It may sound like a lot, but it's not much at all. The only thing I'm going off of is this picture. I'm just trying to put my family's history together.

Lisa: Can I see the picture? If it was taken here I'll know it. I know this town up and down, inside and out. Also what I don't know, which isn't much mind you, you can find in these books here. History records, as far back as they can go.

(Johnathan hands Lisa the picture. Lisa observes it for a second and hands it back.)

Lisa: Oh yeah! That's here alright. That store used to be by the railroad tracks. I don't really recognize his face though. What you say your last name was again honey?

Johnathan: Barnes, ma'am.

Lisa: No, no recollection of any Barnes from around here and trust me, I would know. And your grandfather's name was also Johnathan?

Johnathan: Yes ma'am. And my father and myself.

Lisa: Hmm, nope. Don't know the name. Sorry honey.

(Johnathan walks to the bookshelf and chooses the first book to start his quest.)

Johnathan: I would like to take a look at these records ma'am. I figured I'd have to do some searching anyhow so I traveled early to get here at a good time.

Lisa: I hope you didn't have to travel far. Where you from?

Johnathan: Only a couple of hours away ma'am, just on the other side of the state line.

(Johnathan takes a seat at the table and starts to read.)

Lisa: Well honey, you take your time with those records. But I do need you to keep in mind, young man, that sometime history don't write people down as they are, they write them down as who they decide they should be.

Johnathan: Yes ma'am, I'll keep that in mind.

Lisa: Well then good. And we don't get a lot of visitors here so it'll be nice and quiet for some family searching. With the exception of my brother and his daughter who work next door you're actually the only person I've seen in here this week.

(Harold enters hurriedly from stage right. He startles Lisa.)

Harold: Lisa! Ya got any gas pills?

Lisa: Harold! How many times have I told you about coming through the back door?! You bout scared me half to death!

Harold *(ignoring her)*: My stomach been bubblin' real bad since last night. We aint had no pills at da house and we not stocked up in da sto'. I saw ya bag in da room back there but I ain't wanna go through ya stuff. Ya got any?

(Harold notices Johnathan. He's not embarrassed.)

Harold: I ain't know ya had somebody in hea.

Lisa: I know you heard the bell Harold.

Harold: Well yeah but I din't think nothin' of it. Maybe ya stepped out or somethin'. Ion know.

Lisa: How would I be in here if I stepped out Harold?

Harold: Ya askin' too many questions woman. *(to Johnathan)* Who is you son?

Johnathan: Johnathan, sir.

Harold: Johnathan, sir. Ya got a last name Johnathan, sir?

Johnathan: Barnes, sir. Johnathan Barnes the Third.

Harold: Well Sir Johnathan Barnes sir, nice ta meet ya. Lisa, gas pills?

Lisa: Yes Harold, I have some in my bag. I'll go grab them.

(Lisa exits stage right. Johnathan starts reading through the book.)

Harold: What brings ya ta Ferrum son?

Johnathan: Looking for my family sir.

Harold: Family? What ya say ya name was again? Barnes? Nah ain't no Barneses 'round here. I see ya looking through dem books. Good luck. Lisa don't take care of dem books like she posed to.

(Lisa enters stage right.)

Lisa: Excuse me? I take care of those books just fine. I read them and I put them back. And sometimes I read them again just to keep my memory fresh for when the occasional stranger walks in wanting to know about the history of this wonderful town.

(Lisa hands Harold the gas pills. Harold sits down next to Johnathan.)

Harold: Thank ya kindly. But ya know da reason ya keep readin' dem books is because ya gettin' old and ain't got no man ta tend ta no mo'. Ya ain't got nothin' else ta do.

Lisa: Uh, shouldn't you be taking your butt back to work?

Harold: Is ya in my business? Missy over dere. Pretending ta work. Dat's betta den nothin' I guess. Dat gal dere.

Lisa: Harold, let's not start in front of company.

Harold: All dat gal do is walk around sad and sulkin'. She swea' she so miserable. Ungrateful is mo' like it. Like I told ha ta come back. I ain't tell ha ta come back. If she wanna gon' on then gon' on. Sir Johnathan Barnes sir, you got kids?

(Johnathan, reading, doesn't respond. Harold slaps the table.)

Harold: Sir Johnathan sir!

Johnathan: Huh, what was that? Sorry.

Harold: Kids? Ya got kids?

Johnathan: No sir.

Harold: Save yaself da headache. Especially dem gals. Hard-headed and stubborn.

Lisa: Harold! That's enough.

(The store bell rings. Johnathan looks at the door again. Nothing. Again.)

Harold: Ya lucky I gotta get back. Sir Johnathan Barnes sir, it was nice ta meet ya.

(Harold exits stage right. Lisa is visibly upset.)

Lisa: The nerve of that fool.

(Lisa collects herself.)

Lisa: I'm sorry, honey. My brother and his daughter have a very... "special" relationship. Don't you mind a word he says. So, how about I tell you a bit about our little town's history. I am the official historian after all.

Johnathan: Thank you ma'am, but you don't have to do that. I read the town's Wikipedia page and did a little online research of my own before I came.

Lisa: Oh, how could I ever compete with the town's Wikipedia page? Honey, Lisa Warner-Wilson knows more about this place than any man or machine. You young people and your internet. I bet that internet won't tell you that my great-grandfather was one of the first Black people to own land here did it? Back when Black folks were just trying to survive after they "ended" slavery, my great-grandfather was building generational wealth. He passed down what he learned and earned to my grandfather, Henry Warner, who worked hard and saved every penny he had and bought more land from a white man and built the town's first Black-owned restaurant. Booming business that kept this place relevant for years. I bet the internet didn't tell you that.

Johnathan: Oh no ma'am, it ain't say all that.

Lisa: Of course it didn't honey. I also bet you didn't know that in the early 1900s the Great Migration had a bunch of Black folks, especially younger people, leaving the south. That's probably how your grandfather ended up up north. Our little town was hit pretty hard and the Black population fell way down but then white folks started to leave too.

Johnathan: Wait, wouldn't white people be happy that all the Black people were leaving town? Why would they want to leave as well?

Lisa: Honey if it ain't no Black folk around to do the heavy lifting and bean picking then what the white folks need to stay for? All their workers were leaving to go up North and find better lives and wages than the pennies they were making down here. Yeah, a few of them stayed but eventually the Black people that were left here started to buy up the rest of the white man land and work for themselves. Black folks had finally caught on to what my grandfather and great-grandfather had done. A few family members left Ferrum but the majority of the Warners were born here and most have died here. Yeah, a couple people left but mostly everybody always make their way back home. My mama worked right here at this post office until she retired and then I took over. My grandfather started working here back when the post office was located in the back of a merchandise store before he started his restaurant. I told you he worked hard. It was actually his idea to split this building in two so him and some local town folk put up some walls and now we got ourselves a post office on one side and the old merchandise store is now the town gas station convenience store on the other side. My granddaddy let my daddy take over the gas station. That's how he and my mama met. Then he died and now Harold is running the place over there.

Johnathan: Sounds like your family is pretty important here.

Lisa: We are. As well as the other families around here. Everybody here is a part of our community so there's not one family more important than the other. We're pretty tight knit around here. Our community is really just one big extended family.

Johnathan: So you've never left?

Lisa: I left. For a little while. To go and get educated. My mother's wishes, not mine. But I came right back here because this is home. My brother has never left these city limits. My mama neither. It's safe here. We don't really have to deal with too many OUTSIDERS on the regular.

(Lisa looks Johnathan up and down. He doesn't notice.)

Johnathan: I guess if my roots trace back here then that would make us basically family too, huh.

Lisa: Well I can't say for sure but even if your search turns up unsuccessful you can always call me Auntie Lisa. A lot of the younger people do.

(The store bell rings. Johnathan looks towards the door. Nobody enters.)

Johnathan: Thanks for that. I hope my grandfather's family is half as interesting as yours.

Lisa: If they're from here, I'm sure they are. Black folks roots run deep in this town's history. I can give you more than an earful about this place, that's if you don't mind listening some more, of course.

Johnathan: No ma'am, I don't mind at all.

CURTAIN.

A store counter sits in the corner of the gas station convenience store. A snack stand and table are also present. Behind the counter stands Melissa writing something.

Harold walks in stage left holding his stomach. Melissa doesn't look up.

Harold: Who was dat dat came in hea Missy?

(Melissa looks up and heavy sighs then puts her head down to continues her writing.)

Melissa: Just somebody come by to pay for some gas, why?

Harold: I can't ask who comes in and out of MY store gal?

Melissa: It's your store, you do what you want.

Harold: As long as ya know dat. So I was just next door witcha auntie and it's a nice looking man in dere. Ya need ta go and say hi.

Melissa: And why would I do that dad?

Harold: Because ya ain't gettin' any younga. My mama had both me and Lisa before she turned 30 and hea ya go wasting away ya good years. Gon' over and talk ta dat young man.

(Melissa still doesn't look at her father.)

Melissa: Dad, I'm a lesbian. We've had this discussion. Numerous times actually. Going over there would be a bigger waste of time than me going over this inventory knowing we get about three people in here on a good day.

Harold: Oh yous young people don't know whatcha want. Whatcha need is a man and some babies ta tend ta. Back in my day da woman ran the house and da man worked and came home ta a hot meal at the end of da day. Ya mama, God rest ha soul, she sholl did know how ta be a good woman. She did da best she could with da boys. I don't know what happened wit you.

19

Melissa: Not every woman wants babies dad. And my mama raised me just fine. I just don't want that stereotypical baby on my hip and one in my belly walking around barefoot and pregnant life that you want for me. Is that wrong of me to want to be a woman my own way?

Harold: If ya own way is round here kissing girls den it damn sholl is wrong! Now gon on over dere and talk ta dat young man before Lisa drive him away. Ya know she talk too much. Boy prolly gon be sleepin' when ya get dere. Gon wake him up Missy.

(Melissa stops writing and looks directly at her father.)

Melissa: Unbelievable.

(Melissa storms out stage right. The store bell rings. Harold picks up where Melissa left off with the inventory while humming a familiar tune. Junie Mae enters stage right.)

Harold: Hey mama! Ya just missed Missy. I told ha to gon' ova dere ta talk ta some young fella dat Lisa got ova dere at da mail house.

Junie Mae: I saw Missy, I mean Melissa, run past me with tears in her eyes. Harold, what did you do ta her? Ya always picking on dat gal.

Harold: Aw mama, I ain't did nothin' ta ha. I told ha ta go ova there next door and meet the man Lisa talkin' ta.

Junie Mae: Harold. Your daughter is a lesbian. She like otha women. Why on God's green Earth would you try to push her towards a man?

Harold: Oh not you too mama. A woman can't like no woman. How two womans gon have babies with no man? She need ta get what and who she can and soon. I told ha she ain't gettin' no younga.

Junie Mae: You ain't tell her dat.

Harold: I did and I'd tell ha again. All my boys off and married wit babies and my one girl, my BABY girl, say she don't like men AND she don't want no babies? How is dat 'posed ta make me feel? Everybody else daughtas got babies but my daughter wanna be a man, kissin' on otha girls.

Junie Mae: Da nerve of you! When ya got sick dat child gave up ha life ta come back home and take care of ya. If ya daddy were alive he'd slap da taste outcha mouth for da way ya talk about ha.

Harold: Y'all da ones dat wanted Missy back hea. I ain't ask ha ta come back, daddy ain't here, and sorry mama but dat's my child, not yerrs.

Junie Mae: And I'm ya mama and don't ya ever forget that. Ya know how many times dat child come ta me crying? More den enough.

(Junie Mae looks around.)

Junie Mae: Ya done made me forget why I came in here.

Harold: Dat's because ya old mama. Ya ain't even supposed to be out da house.

Junie Mae: I walked here for something but now I forgot Harold. Oh, what was it?

Harold: Some chips mama? We ain't got much here. Unless ya need some gas.

Junie Mae: I said I walked boy. Don't be stupid. I'll just get some candy den.

(Junie Mae grabs a candy bar and heads towards the door.)

Harold: Mama! You owe me a dollar twenty fa dat candy. You can't just walk in and outta here takin' stuff and not payin' fa it!

Junie Mae: *(walking out)* Watch ya tone boy! Don't ya forget who put ya in dis place. Talking about I can't take stuff. Tuh. I'll take all da stuff!

(Junie Mae exits stage right. The store bell rings.)

Harold *(shaking his head):* Dese women round here don't respect nobody.

(Harold goes back to humming his familiar tune. Beat. The store bell rings. Lisa enters stage right.)

Harold: Lisa, what ya doing in here? I just sent Missy over dere to see ya.

Lisa: Melissa didn't come by. What you send her over that way for?

(Lisa grabs a bag of chips and starts to eat them.)

Harold: What is wrong wit yall women today!? Mama came in here and did da same thang! Respect my space!

Lisa: Oh shut up Harold.

Harold: Disrespectful, all of ya. Anyway. I sent Missy over dere ta meet dat boy Sir Johnathan. He gone?

Lisa: No, he's still there. Reading. I gave him some time to himself so I can come talk to you about dinner. I'm thinking about making hibachi instead of meatloaf and potatoes tonight!

(Harold looks at her dumbfounded.)

Harold: Woman what da hell wrong witcha!? Ya left dat boy ova dere by hisself? What if he steal sum'n? And hibachi? How you gon make some hibachi, ya ain't neva eva made hibachi befo'. Hell, ya ain't neva even HAD hibachi befo'. Stop playin' woman. All y'all women crazy today! You, mama, and Missy too!

Lisa; What's he gonna steal Harold? Some mail? He looks like a kind boy that's just trying to find out what he can and be on his way.

Smart boy, but he moves fast like he has to know everything right now.

Harold: Well I hope he don't move too fast. I'm tryna get Missy ta see him. He might knock some sense in ha head. Dat's a good looking boy. Dey would make nice looking babies too.

Lisa: What are you talking about? Melissa is gay. And you know she hates when you call her Missy.

Harold: Well when she was my baby girl she loved bein' called Missy so I call ha Missy.

Lisa: She ain't a baby no more. The sooner you understand that, the easier it'll be to accept it. But anyway, what do I know?

Harold: Nothin' because ya ain't got no kids.

(Lisa ignores him and changes the subject.)

Lisa: So I guess hibachi is out of the question huh? That's got a lot of sodium and it was gonna take too long anyway.

Harold: Ya aight, dat's da reason.

Lisa: Well look. Every last Friday it's the same thing. Meatloaf and potatoes. We've been eating meatloaf and potatoes every last Friday since we were kids, without fail. I've been thinking about this all day and I think it's time for a change.

Harold: Ya ain't changin' nothin' Lisa. The last Friday of the month is meatloaf and potatoes day.

Lisa: You mean to tell me you still want meatloaf and potatoes after all this time?

Harold: I do.

Lisa: You don't.

Harold: I do and mama do too.

Lisa: Well I'm gonna ask mama and see what she say. She prolly won't even care.

Harold: Of course she gon' care. It's ha rule. Just cuz she old don't mean she gon' change ha rule. She might not rememba a whole lot but she rememba ha meatloaf and potatoes on da last Friday.

Lisa: Well maybe I'll just make it a surprise then. Plus what can she really do if we don't have meatloaf and potatoes? She ain't cooked in years so she's just gonna have to eat whatever I make.

Harold: Ha! Gal ya done bumped ya head tuhday?

Lisa: Yeah we'll see. How much I owe you for the chips?

Harold

I normally would charge ya but ya need ta get on back ova dere before you get back and all ya stamps gone right along wit Sir Johnathan sir. Walk in and its envelopes and package tape all on da ground.

Lisa: Oh hush up Harold. The boy is fine, plus you right next door if something happens. I'm bout to go see mama. You think she home?

Harold: Prolly. She came in hea and left right befo' ya came in.

Lisa: She say where she was going?

Harold: Naw, she din't. She prolly went home doe. She say she forgot why she came here so she prolly just went back to where she know.

Lisa: *(walking out)* Poor mama. I'm about to head over there now. Don't be surprised when we're not eating meatloaf and potatoes tonight.

Harold: Yeah aight. We gon' see.

(Lisa exits stage right.)

CURTAIN.

Johnathan is sitting reading through a book in the post office. The store bell rings. Melissa hurriedly enters stage left.

Melissa: Auntie Lisa I need you to talk, or knock, your preference, some sense into my dad. I can't take it anymore!

(Melissa notices Johnathan.)

Melissa: You're not Auntie Lisa.

Johnathan: I'm not. My name is Johnathan. Barnes the Third.

Melissa: Oh you must be the guy my dad is trying to hook me up with.

Johnathan: I would ask who your dad is but there's only been one other man in here today and he seems like the hook 'em up type.

Melissa: Yeah, we don't get a lot of visitors here. Do you know where my Auntie Lisa went?

Johnathan: She said she had to go talk to someone about dinner. I really wasn't listening when she left, sorry. She just told me to make sure I don't leave but I have no intention to until I find what I'm looking for.

Melissa: And exactly what are you looking for? I'm Melissa by the way.

Johnathan: Nice to meet you Melissa. I'm searching for records of my grandfather. I found a picture that was taken here mixed in with my father's things. I asked him about it, he said the only thing he knew about his father was that he gave him his name and he was born in the south. Google didn't tell me much so I decided to come here in person to find out what I can.

Melissa: That's a very millennial thing of you to do. You must not have a girlfriend. Or... boyfriend?

Johnathan: Oh, sorry. I'm taken.

Melissa: Don't be. I'm gay.

Johnathan: Oh... that's cool.

Melissa: So you found this picture. Drove here. And now you're looking through old records to see if you can find information about your grandfather. Because you didn't have anything else to do on a Friday.

Johnathan: No, but also yes. Hey, do you happen to know if there's any digital versions of these books anywhere? All these pages are making my eyes hurt.

Melissa: That's a negative. Unfortunately Ferrum is nowhere near that advanced. Also don't even think of asking for the Wi-Fi password. It doesn't exist. There is no Wi-Fi. This entire raggedy town needs an upgrade. But don't tell the elders that.

Johnathan: The elders?

Melissa: My dad, Auntie Lisa, my grandma. All the old people. The elders.

Johnathan: Ah, yes. Of course, the elders.

Melissa: Everything has been the same since I was born. Literally. Got the baby pictures to prove it. Same buildings, same roads, same town.

Johnathan: You been here your whole life? That sounds interesting.

Melissa: I left. For college. Graduated last semester.

Johnathan: And you decided to come back here?

Melissa: Family issues.

Johnathan: Fair enough.

Melissa: To be honest though, I've had my bags packed ready to leave again for a few days now. For good this time. I won't be coming back if I do.

Johnathan: If. Your family issues gone?

Melissa: No. But I don't think my dad would even care if I left.

Johnathan: Then leave.

Melissa: It's not always that easy.

Johnathan: It is though. Just like how I came here. You just do it.

Melissa: Yeah okay.

(Melissa grabs a random book.)

Melissa: You wanna know what's funny? I've never actually read these books.

Johnathan: Never?

Melissa: Yeah, I never cared to. Like I know my family history traces back to slavery or something but nothing around here ever changes so I feel like I would just be looking at old pictures of the same buildings.

Johnathan: Oh, it's so much more than pictures. The years are by tens, to match up with the census archives. That's what I'm looking at, the census stuff. The latest records available are from 1950 because of the 72 year rule so I started there and have been working my way backwards. Nothing so far. By the way, your aunt actually has these record books really organized.

(Johnathan puts the book back on the shelf and grabs the next book to read. Melissa is mentally in her own world. Beat.)

Melissa: So do you really think I should leave?

Johnathan: If leaving makes you happy, then leave.

Melissa: I should leave. I mean, it's not like my dad is going to miss me. Yeah grandma and Auntie Lisa will, but they'll be fine right?

Johnathan: Right, of course. That's why we have phones. And FaceTime.

Melissa: *(confidently)* I think I'm going to leave.

(Johnathan flips frantically through the book he's holding.)

Johnathan: And I think that your aunt isn't as good with these records as I thought. The 1890 census is missing.

(Johnathan quickly skims through the remaining books on the shelf.)

Melissa: It has to be here somewhere. My aunt prolly just misplaced it. Just skip it and go to the next census.

Johnathan: *(getting quickly annoyed)*: No, no, no, I can't "just skip it and go to the next census." Google says this town wasn't incorporated until 1886, so in 1880 they wouldn't even be listed under this name. *(resigned)* That's as far back as I can go.

(Johnathan slams the book down.)

Melissa: I mean there has to be somewhere else to look then, right? Maybe outside of the census records. Just relax.

Johnathan: Don't tell me to relax. I've been in here for a while now and I've come up with nothing. There isn't a Barnes in any of these books anywhere.

Melissa: Somebody's being dramatic.

Johnathan *(with growing frustration)*: You're calling me dramatic and you don't even know me. This is important.

Melissa: I'm just saying. Plus it's not like it's that big of a deal if you do find what you're looking for or if you don't. You're not going to have some life changing experience just because your family may or may not be from this terrible little town.

Johnathan: You have your entire family's history right here at your fingertips. You can pick up any of these books and go back at least a few generations, but you haven't because you never cared to. You know where you're from. I'm literally chasing a picture here. Some of us aren't afforded the luxury of just knowing where we're from. We can't just walk down the same streets of those that came before us.

Melissa *(talking loudly)*: You think this is luxury? Imagine. Knowing your people have been living here for years. Years. As far back as our history shows us. Just for this place to be the same way it's been since we were brought here. Nothing changes here. This isn't a place to be proud of. Being from this place, living here and this life. Getting away from it and coming right back to it because apparently people here can't live life without you. Nothing about any of this is a luxury. If it is, then you can have it and I'll take your life. The life where you can just get up and go. Without having to worry about anyone but yourself. Must be nice.

Johnathan *(yelling)*: LEAVE! If life is so bad here then go! I see why your dad came in here complaining. You ARE ungrateful!

(Beat.)

Melissa: ... my dad said what?

(Harold enters stage right.)

Harold: What's all dat noise going on ova hea'? I heard y'all way from the sto'.

Melissa: You called me ungrateful?

Harold: Yea, prolly. Why?

Melissa: You are truly unbelievable. I'm ungrateful!? *(yelling at her father)* I came back here FOR YOU! YOU got sick and needed help! I was fine on my own, living my life not having to suffocate myself in this sinkhole of a town. But no, *(imitating her grandmother)* "ya daddy on his deathbed. Come on home gal!"

Harold: Mind ya elder now Missy! I'on know who ya think ya yellin' at and I ain't tell you or mama I needed help! Y'all decided dat

29

on ya own. I'on need ya. Gon' on den if ya wanna leave, shit. I'll help ya pack!

Melissa: I never should've come back here.

(The store bell rings. Lisa enters stage left.)

Lisa: Oh Harold, Melissa, what y'all doing over here? Who's running next door?

Harold: I was ova dere befo' I heard Missy-

Melissa: And stop calling me Missy! You know how much I hate that and you still do it like my feelings don't matter, but no surprise there right dad? (mockingly) I's sholl don't care bout nothin' but myself. I don't need nobody to help me. Only sickness round here is the sickness that took ova my daughta' that make ha kiss otha women.

(Harold is visibly upset. He paces back and forth.)

Harold: Now Missy, I done told you bout that mouth of yours. Keep-

Melissa: *(interrupting and still mocking him)*: Now hold on now Missy. I done told you bout that-

(Harold lunges at Melissa, but Johnathan quickly restrains him. Harold tries unsuccessfully to get out of the restraint.)

Harold: Get ya hands off me boy! *(to Melissa)* I told ya ta watch ya mouth Missy. Ya need ta show some respect! *(to Johnathan)* I said let me go!

Lisa: Harold!

Melissa: Nah, let him go!

Johnathan: I'm sorry but I can't do that.

(Harold struggles to get loose. Melissa walks up to him.)

Melissa: I hope you die.

(Melissa exits stage left. The store bell rings. Johnathan lets Harold go.)

Harold: What's wrong wit da gal? Everybody done went damn crazy tuhday?

Lisa: Harold, what did you do to her?

Johnathan: Hi. Ms. Lisa, sorry to interrupt. But it looks like some records are missing?

Lisa: Give me a minute to talk to my brother, honey. This is important.

Johnathan: I hear you ma'am, and I understand that. It's just that I really need to know where these records are.

Harold: Damn boy, din't she say not now?

Johnathan *(getting frustrated)*: Ma'am, sir, this is important to me.

Harold: And dis important to us. You can wait. So anyway. Missy decided-

(Johnathan can no longer hold in his frustration.)

Johnathan *(interrupting)*: But the thing is sir, is that I can't wait. I've been here for a while now. I've been patient, I've been respectful, I didn't move a muscle when I was in here alone. I've sat through and listened to much more dysfunction than I thought I would today...

(The store bell rings. No one is there.)

Johnathan: ... and that store bell has been ringing all day! I know you all hear it because I hear it and no one seems to mind nor care!

(Johnathan calms himself down.)

Johnathan: I'm sorry.

Harold: Yep I'm out. Everybody done lost dey damn minds tuhday. And it ain't just da womens eitha.

(Harold exits stage right. Lisa is speechless.)

Johnathan: I'm so sorry ma'am. This is just really important to me and I-

Lisa *(interrupting him)*: Young man, I think it's time for you to leave. Thank you for visiting Ferrum. I hope you found what you were looking for. Please put everything back where you found it and leave. Have a safe trip home.

(Lisa exits stage right. Johnathan is left alone and disappointed, mainly in himself.)

CURTAIN.

Lisa and Harold are sitting in the gas station convenience store.

Harold: I don't know what's gotten into errbody tuhday. These chillun done lost dey damn minds. Who dat boy think he is raisin' his voice? And, and Missy? She lucky sir Johnathan sir was in between us cuz she almost got knocked upside da damn head. Let ha try it again. I'm tellin' ya Lisa.

Lisa: You know Harold I try to be a good person, you know?

Harold: Oh Lisa, don't let da boy get ta ya. Ya know ya a good person.

Lisa: I try to be helpful, you know? He came asking questions and I tried to help as much as I could. Even gave him some alone time to really get into what he was looking for. And for him to just yell at me like that? Like I'm the worst person ever.

Harold: Nobody thinks ya da worst person. Looks like da boy just got frustrated. Ya know dese kids. Wit all the emotion and whatnot. Ya know, soft.

Lisa: Ungrateful is more like it. Like I owed it to him to stop in the middle of what I'm doing to tend to his needs.

Harold: Dat's just kids period Lisa. Dey take what dey want and talk ta ya any ol' kinda way. Like Missy. Who she think she is? She wish I die. If I die, den what? She gon' be happy I bet. If I drop dead right now she gon' prolly dance ova my body.

Lisa: You know she didn't mean that. She was just angry. I mean you did try to attack her.

Harold: Ain't nobody attackin' nobody. She started talkin' crazy so I got crazy right back with ha. I want her ta try it again doe. Dat boy ain't gon be there again to save ha next time.

33

Lisa: He sure won't. I sent him home.

Harold: Ya sent da boy home? Why ya do dat Lisa?

Lisa: What do you mean why? You saw how he talked to me.

Harold: Da boy been in dere all day lookin' through dem books. Head prolly hurtin' then here we come wit some mess. He got a lil' mad but dat ain't a reason ta kick him out. He tryna find his family ain't it? Dat ain't right ta kick da boy out when he just tryna find where his family from Lisa.

Lisa: With him it's compassion, but with your daughter it's anger. Explain that one Harold.

Harold: Ah Lisa, boys will be boys. Men get hot headed sometimes. We calm down soon after. Don't mean no harm to nobody.

Lisa: And women aren't afforded the same sympathy?

Harold: Women say what dey mean. Y'all think too much ta let just anythang come out ya mouths.

Lisa: Whatever Harold. Anyway, he's gone now and it's getting close to dinner time. Oh, I went by mama's earlier. She said she wasn't feeling too well so I didn't stay too long but I did tell her I'm making a surprise for dinner.

Harold: A surprise? Woman ya done lost it. What she say? I know she said somethin'.

Lisa: She said that sounds good.

Harold: You know she ain't meant that. Mama gettin' old Lisa.

Lisa: I know she's getting older, which is probably why she's letting me make something different for our monthly meal tonight. You know what? Let me stop wasting time here and go clean up the mess the boy made next door, because I'm sure he didn't clean up his mess before he left, and go over to mama's to start cooking.

Harold: Whatcha gon' make?

Lisa: I don't know yet, maybe it'll be a surprise to me too!

Harold: Oh mama ain't gon' like dat at all. Good luck!

(The store bell rings. Melissa enters stage right.)

Harold: What you doin' hea Missy? Don't come in hea startin' no mo' stuff.

Melissa: Aunt Lisa, you mind if I talk to my dad alone?

Lisa: Sure honey, I was just leaving. See y'all at mama house later.

(Lisa exits stage right. The store bell rings.)

Harold: I don't know why dat woman won't just go through the back ta da mail house. She always walk all da way around. Fa what? I'll never know. Anyway, what ya want Missy?

Melissa: First off, dad, I came to apologize. I said I wish you'd die and I don't mean that. I was upset and I'm adult enough to admit when I'm wrong so I'm sorry.

Harold: Ya came up in hea ta tell me dat? I know'd you ain't mean it, what ya thank I'm stupid? Huh Missy?

Melissa: Second, I came to ask that you stop calling me Missy. I don't like that name. I've asked you before and you completely ignored me. I haven't liked that name in a long time.

Harold: It's ya name. I gave ya that name when ya was a baby. It used ta make you smile.

Melissa: It did. When I was a kid. It doesn't anymore. Now it just feels like you only call me Missy to make sure that I know I'm still your little girl.

Harold: And what's wrong wit dat? Ya still is my li'l gal and ya name gon be Missy til I can't talk no mo'.

35

Melissa: Do you hear yourself right now? I'm asking for one thing from you. That's it. Just one thing. And you can't even respect my wishes.

Harold: Respect ya wishes? What I look like a genie in a bottle?

Melissa: I don't know why I came back here. You know, I try to be the bigger person. I try and try with you and you're so stuck in your ways that you can't even see how awful you make me feel.

Harold: Ya feel awful, ya feelings don't matter, ya tryna be da bigga person. It ain't always about you Missy.

Melissa: It's never about me! Ever. It's always about you.

Harold: Me!? Ain't nothin' round hea eva about me. Don't nobody care about what Harold want.

Melissa: I don't care what you want because you want me to be someone that I'm not.

Harold: What? A woman? You want me to happy that you don't want to be a woman?

Melissa: Who said I don't want to be a woman dad? I am a woman. Just because I don't fit into your stereotypical box of what I "should" be doesn't make me any less of a woman.

Harold: I don't see how ya gon' be a real woman likin' otha women. I don't know what happened up at that college. Ya went ta school likin' boys and ya come back likin' girls.

Melissa: You can't be serious.

Harold: I told mama letting ya leave this town wasn't a good idea. Now look at ya.

(Melissa is speechless. Beat.)

Harold: Well don't just stand there wit ya mouth wide open. Help me clean up so I can get some rest befo' I head to mama house.

Melissa: Do you really hate me that much?

Harold: Oh hea we go again wit da feelins. What ya want me to say Missy? *(mockingly)* Oh I love you so much Melissa. Of course I don't hate ya for not giving me grandchildren or hell even a son-in-law. I love ya pissy attitude and how ya hate everything. My favorite part of the day is watching ya hate being here with me when I didn't have to give ya a job. I just love it all so much.

(Melissa storms out stage right. The store bell rings.)

Junie Mae *(offstage)*: What's wrong Missy, I mean Melissa? Melissa? Melissa, come back!

(Junie Mae enters stage right.)

Junie Mae: Now dis the second time dis week dat gal done ran past me.

Harold: This week? Mama dat happened earlier today.

Junie Mae: Don't sass me boy. What ya keep doing ta my grandbaby Harold?

Harold: I ain't doin' nothin' ta nobody. Why I always gotta be da one doin' somethin'?

Junie Mae: Shut up. You know you always messin' with everybody.

Harold: Ain't gon be too many mo' shut ups mama.

Junie Mae: Melissa done got ya chest all puffed out and now ya think ya can talk to me crazy?

Harold: Nah, it ain't like that at all. It's just a respect thang. That's all mama.

Junie Mae: So now I don't respect ya?

Harold: I ain't say that mama. What ya doin' back here anyway? The sun gon' be goin' down soon.

Junie Mae: What dat mean? I walk around town all da time, day and night.

Harold: I know mama, but ya gettin' older and me and Lisa think-

Junie Mae: Y'all think what? Dat I can't take care of myself? I can take care of myself. Why you think I came down here? Because I'm taking care of myself.

Harold: Alright mama, what ya need now?

Junie Mae: ... I can't remember. It was somethin' I need.

Harold: Was it something fa dinner?

Junie Mae: What I'm gon' get from a gas station for dinner Harold?

Harold: Maybe some drinks or something I don't know. Lisa said she making a surprise tonight. Ya okay with dat mama?

Junie Mae: Okay with what?

Harold: Lisa makin' somethin' special fa dinner later.

Junie Mae: What's later?

Harold: Our monthly Friday dinner? Tuhnight? At yo house?

Junie Mae: We can't be having dinner at my house tonight. Lisa say she wanna make a surprise so tuhday can't be Friday because she know we do meatloaf and potatoes on da last Friday.

Harold: Lisa said she was gonna talk to ya about trying something different instead of meatloaf.

Junie Mae: She can try whatever she want but if we doing dinner at my house den we gon' be having meatloaf. Now I gotta go to da grocery store. Gotta get MY meatloaf started in case ya crazy sister try to serve us some rabbit food for dinner.

Harold: She said she gonna make some hibachi.

Junie Mae: Some what?

Harold: Hibachi.

Junie Mae: What the hell is a habitchy? Oh no, let me get out of here.

Harold: Okay mama. You need me ta walk you?

Junie Mae: You think I can't walk myself across town? What you think I'm handicap?

Harold: Nah mama, I was just askin'.

Junie Mae: Don't talk to me any ol' kind of way Harold.

Harold: I'm not, I was just- never mind. Let me at least walk you out mama.

(Harold and Junie Mae exit stage right. The store bell rings.)

CURTAIN.

The store bell rings. Lisa enters stage left. She notices that Johnathan didn't clean up before he left. Books are everywhere.

Lisa: I asked the boy to do one thing before he leaves. Did he do it? Of course not.

(Lisa cleans up the mess Johnathan left out. The store bell rings. Johnathan enters stage left.)

Johnathan: Ms. Lisa?

(Lisa stares at him but does not answer.)

Johnathan: Auntie Lisa?

(Johnathan makes an awkward Kawhi Leonard laugh sound.)

Lisa *(dryly)*: Can I help you?

Johnathan I was just about to head out of town when I realized that I hadn't cleaned up. So, I turned around. And also, I'm sorry. It's been a long day and I got so caught up, and you were being dismissive... I'm sorry.

Lisa: You yelled at me. Nobody yells at me.

Johnathan: I raised my voice. I'm sorry.

(Lisa ignores his apology.)

Lisa: Try it again and see what happen. I don't take too kindly to folks, especially strangers, yelling at me.

Johnathan: I won't.

Lisa: I know you won't. Anyway, you said that something was missing?

Johnathan: Oh yeah, right. So I couldn't find the census records from 1890.

Lisa: Oh, well that's because there are no census records from 1890.

Johnathan: What?

Lisa: I know you heard me because you responded. *(talking slower)* There are no census records from 1890.

Johnathan: What do you mean there are no census records from 1890. How does that happen?

Lisa: I'm sorry honey, but that's something you're going to have to take up with the U.S. government.

Johnathan: I don't understand.

Lisa: Oh of course you don't. Sit down, let me teach you something else today.

(Lisa and Johnathan sit down.)

Lisa: So. First, let's address this. Don't you ever be disrespectful to me again. I know your parents did not raise you that way.

Johnathan: I'm sorry ma'am I-

Lisa *(interrupting)*: Do not interrupt me right now young man.

(Johnathan zips his mouth shut.)

Lisa: Second, we don't have the 1890 census records because the 1890 census records do not exist for this town.

Johnathan: What do you mean they don't-

(Lisa turns her head sharply and gives Johnathan "the look".)

Johnathan: Sorry.

(Lisa shakes her head.)

Lisa: A good bit of the 1890 census records for this town, this state and a large majority of the rest of the entire country was damaged in a fire in the Commerce Building in Washington, DC in 1921. Water damage and whatnot from some firemen messed up a lot more of it. Then the messed up sections were destroyed some years later because some high up government folks decided it wasn't worth trying to salvage.

Johnathan: They just destroyed them? Just like that?

Lisa: Just like that honey.

Johnathan: Wow. That's really messed up when you think about it.

Lisa *(sarcastically)*: Ya think?

(Johnathan misses the sarcasm.)

Johnathan: Yeah I do. Like think about it. These were people's ancestors. And that information is just gone. And there's nothing that we can do about it. It's sad really.

Lisa: Yes, it is, but you know it's just another one of the realities we face as Black people. A lot of people have no idea where they came from and there is no clear cut way to figure it out. I applaud you for your journey young man, even if things don't turn out how you think they're going to.

Johnathan: I don't think they will ma'am. That 1890 census record could've answered a lot of questions for me.

Lisa: How so?

Johnathan: Well, Google said the city was incorporated in 1886 so there wouldn't be any local census records from here before 1890. Those were the last records my grandfather or his family could've been in.

Lisa: While that may be true, there should still be other places you can look outside of the census records.

Johnathan: That's what Melissa was trying to tell me too. I need to find her and apologize too.

Lisa: Apologize for what?

Johnathan: ... yelling at her.

Lisa: Oh so yelling is something you do often.

Johnathan: No ma'am it's not, I can just be really passionate when it comes to things I care about.

Lisa: Well honey, I know I told you to leave but you know you don't really have to leave.

Johnathan: Actually ma'am I think I do. I feel like my presence here disturbed what would've been just a normal day for you all and I don't want to continue to make it more awkward by sticking around.

Lisa: Oh honey, please. Families bicker and argue all the time. At the end of the day, we're all still family. You don't have to leave on account of us.

Johnathan: I know but I think it's best just to go. Plus it's starting to get late and I don't want to be on the road at night somewhere I don't know. I'm just going to go find Melissa and then I'll be out of here. It was nice meeting you ma'am.

(Johnathan reaches in for a hug with Lisa. She resists, but then obliges.)

Lisa: Well, it was nice to meet you too, young man. You're welcome back here anytime. And maybe next time you come back we can do a little bit of digging together to find where your folks are from.

Johnathan: Sure, ma'am. Next time.

(As Johnathan is about to leave, the store bell rings. Melissa enters stage left. Her and Johnathan have an awkward staring contest.)

Lisa: Alright well, I'll get out of here and give you two some time to talk. Melissa baby, don't forget about dinner at mama's tonight. Oh Johnathan, I wish you weren't leaving so suddenly. Mama would've loved to have met you.

Melissa: What? No she wouldn't have. She don't even like people.

Lisa: That's not true. She doesn't trust people. She can not trust you and like you at the same time. I'm sure she wouldn't have minded. Plus I'm making something special for dinner tonight.

(Melissa laughs.)

Melissa: Special? What, you adding gravy to the meatloaf this time? Because I know you don't think grandma gonna let you serve anything but meatloaf and potatoes tonight.

Lisa: I'm grown! Mama don't tell me what to cook. I cook, y'all eat.

Melissa: You right. You do cook. Meatloaf on the last Fridays.

Johnathan: Man, old…er people must love meatloaf and potatoes because my father has that same tradition. I remember since I was a little boy. The last Friday of every month he'd always make the same thing. Meatloaf and potatoes. I got tired of it as I got older but that was his thing, without fail. A lot of things in life aren't guaranteed, but I can guarantee my father has his meatloaf and potatoes on the last Friday of the month. Every month. He told me his mama, my grandma, used to do the same for him. Apparently my grandfather was a really good cook and that's the one memory of my grandfather she made sure to hold on to and wanted to make sure to pass it to my dad. *(checks watch)* He's probably getting ready to put it in the oven right now.

Lisa: My mother has been making us the same last Friday meal since we were kids and I have been sick of it for the past 30 years. But, like you said it is a tradition. *(sighs heavily)* I guess we're having meatloaf and potatoes tonight. Let me get on over there and get it started. Johnathan, again honey the invitation is open.

Johnathan: Thanks Ms. Lisa. You take care.

Lisa: You do the same.

(Lisa exits stage left. The store bell rings.)

Johnathan: Okay so I was wrong. I shouldn't have yelled at you. That's my fault.

Melissa: That's right. It was your fault.

Johnathan: I know. I just said that. Anyway, I just wanted to-

(Johnathan is interrupted by the store bell. He looks towards the door. Nothing.)

Johnathan: Alright, what's up with the bell? Because this has been driving me nuts all day.

Melissa: What do you mean?

Johnathan: What do you mean what do I mean? You don't hear the store bell ring and then nobody comes in? I mean is it a wire problem that nobody wants to fix? It's been like that all day long.

Melissa: Oh that? That's just people going in and out of my dad's store next door.

Johnathan: Why does this bell ring when that store door is opened?

Melissa: Because this post office and that store used to be one big building. Until they-

Johnathan *(interrupting)*: Put up a wall to split the building in two.

Melissa: Well if you knew, why'd you ask?

Johnathan: I didn't know, at least I didn't realize I knew. Your aunt was talking to me about it earlier but it didn't seem important so I forgot about it. But why not get their own separate store bells?

Melissa: No need to fix what ain't broken.

Johnathan: True, I guess. Well that makes a lot more sense than faulty wiring. At least I know I'm not crazy now.

Melissa: Mmm. I don't know. You were a little crazy for yelling at me when I was just trying to help you.

Johnathan: You're right. Again, sorry about that. I appreciate you trying to help though. And you never know, you could be right. Maybe I'll come back in town and I'll actually take your advice next time.

Melissa: Wait, you're leaving?

Johnathan: Yeah, I was just on my way out when you walked in. Wait, why did you walk in?

Melissa: I came to give you the chance to apologize... and to talk about my dad. I went over there to be the bigger person and it blew up in my face. You're the only one I told I wanted to leave, which is weird because you're a complete stranger, but I needed to talk because I really just don't want to feel this smothered feeling of being stuck here. I really think I want to leave.

Johnathan: I really think you should. Look I've known you all of a day and I can tell that you're unhappy here. You gotta do what's best for you at the end of the day and right now you're doing what's best for everybody else.

Melissa: Yeah you're right.

Johnathan: Yeah, I know I am. But seriously, folks our age? We got too much of life left to live. You could be out exploring the world, but instead you're here with the permanent frumpy face. Because why? Your dad that disrespects you in front of strangers needs help? Nah. That ain't it.

Melissa: Yeah... you're right again. Welp, that's all the motivation I needed. I'm gonna tell my family tonight at dinner. Sure you don't want some meatloaf and potatoes?

Johnathan: No ma'am, I don't.

Melissa: Your loss. It really is good. Our family recipe is undefeated.

Johnathan: I don't know about that one. I never said my grandma's meatloaf was nasty, I just got tired of it. The taste was immaculate though. Second to none.

Melissa: Second to one, you mean. Our recipe is top tier. Can't get any better than a Warner family meatloaf.

Johnathan: I guess I'll have to take your word for it. Like I was telling your aunt, I'm about to get out of here. Gotta stop by your dad's to get some gas and then I'll be on the road. Gotta go before it gets too dark.

Melissa: What you scared of? The boogey man?

Johnathan: Uh yeah, actually. I am. I don't know these roads. Or this town. One stretch to get here took me 40 minutes on a road that has only one lane going both ways and I know they don't have streetlights on them. These country backroads look real boogeyman-ish at night.

Melissa: I can see that. Yeah, you might wanna gon' ahead and go.

Johnathan: Right. I'm about to go gas up and get out. Don't want no issues. It was nice meeting you though Melissa. Maybe I'll see you outside this town one day.

Melissa: Yeah, maybe one day.

(Johnathan exits stage left. The store bell rings. Beat. The store bell rings again. Johnathan re-enters.)

Johnathan *(laughing)*: Ha. The bell. I can't believe I didn't make it make sense earlier. Ah, I'm an idiot. Okay, I'm leaving for real this time.

(Johnathan exits stage left again. The store bell rings.)

CURTAIN.

Harold is sweeping up the store, ready to close for the day. The store bell rings.

Harold: We closed.

(Johnathan enters stage right. Harold doesn't look up.)

Harold: I said we closed, can't ya hear?

Johnathan: Mr. Harold, it's me Johnathan.

Harold: I don't care if it was President Barack Obama, when I say we closed dat mean we closed. Forgot ta lock da damn door.

(Johnathan and Harold awkwardly stare at each other.)

Harold: Oh fine Sir Johnathan, what ya want?

(Harold puts down the broom and heads for the store counter.)

Johnathan: I just need to get some gas before I head out.

Harold: Head out? It's gettin' a lil' late ta be headin' out. You from close by?

Johnathan: Just on the other side of the state line sir.

Harold: Well it might not be too late then. But it could be. You never know. You might as well stay fa dinna' since you still here. I bet Missy want ya ta come ta dinna'.

Johnathan: Are you serious right now?

Harold: Whatcha talkin' bout?

Johnathan; Are you seriously still trying to hook me up with your daughter?

Harold: Ain't nobody tryna hook up nobody. But what if I was?

Johnathan: No offense Mr. Harold, but you gotta do better.

Harold: Ha ha. Says who? You? Sir Johnathan? Y'all young people somethin' else.

49

Johnathan: Look sir, I don't want to be all up in your business but-

Harold: Why people always say dat right befo' dey get up in yo business?

Johnathan: Your daughter hates it here. And she's on the borderline of hating you.

Harold: Why everybody think I care about dat girl hating me? I don't care if Missy hate me! I'm da daddy, not her or y'all.

Johnathan: You know what, sir, you are so right. I didn't even come in here for that. I just came to get some gas so if I could get $30 on pump... what number is that?

(Johnathan looks stage right before continuing conversation with Harold.)

Johnathan: Four please.

Harold: Why people don't pay attention ta dey pump numba? Ya just get out da car and walk right in, don't look at nothin'.

Johnathan: Today I learned twice that I am not very attentive and that is completely my fault. My bad.

Harold: And why y'all young people always thank y'all can give unwanted advice to people y'all don't even know? I know me and Missy ain't got da best relationship but that ain't nobody business but me and hers.

Johnathan: You are so right. About that gas though?

Harold: Don't interrupt me boy, I'm havin' a moment.

(Johnathan zips his lips.)

Harold: People thank I don't know that I'm hard on Missy. I mean Melissa, since she wanna be grown. I know I'm hard on ha. But she gon' have ta get used ta it if she wants to be dis boy version of herself in da rest of da world. We ain't come from da big city. Dis town we in is all of what Melissa know, wit da exception of dem years in college which I objected ta by da way. What she

50

needed ta go ta college fa? And look where she end up. Right back hea. Waste of four and a half years. She could've been here the whole time instead of off halfway cross da country at a school. But if she wanna leave again, I ain't gon' stop ha. She grown and gon do what she want anyway. She should've stayed away if she was gon' stay away. Don't leave and den come back all unhappy.

Johnathan: If you missed her, just say that.

Harold: Don't sass me boy.

(Johnathan zips his lips shut again.)

Harold: Of course I missed ha. I hate how she went to school Missy and came back Melissa. Now look, she all emotional and liking girls. I want my Missy back.

Johnathan: Well how is that fair to her? She went to college and found herself. No offense, but staying here your whole life can't be good for you. No offense. Again.

Harold: So ya sayin' I ain't no good? I ain't left these city limits a day in my life and ya sayin' dat's bad fa me boy?

Johnathan: I said no offense. Twice.

Harold: Dat don't mean nothin'. People always say no offense and den just offense away. Bein' here my whole life been good fa me and ev'rybody round me. Lisa left fa school and left me here. She come back and now she smarter than ev'rybody. Missy did the same thang. I been right here the whole time. Workin' hard and takin' care of my family. Just like all the Warner men. Da men in my family work hard. We don't go off to nobody fancy school. Fa what? We gon end up right back here workin' the same job we was gon' work if we didn't leave. No, the Warner men we stay and we work.

Johnathan: Is that how you got sick?

Harold: Sick!? Ain't nobody sick. I'm just getting olda boy, I'm not unwell.

Johnathan: I'm sorry, everybody kept saying you were sick.

Harold: Dat's all dat women talk. Soft. Dat's all dat is.

Johnathan: It seems like you have a lot of people that care about you and your non-sickness.

Harold: Dey care because ain't no otha man around to take care of em. A woman need a man. Look at my mama. My daddy took care of ha until da day he died. Now look at Lisa. And Missy. Both of em ain't got no man so they round hea worryin' bout me. I can take care of myself.

Johnathan: Can you though?

Harold: Damn right I can. Who gon' tell me I can't?

Johnathan: Nobody I guess. Y'all take card here? I really gotta hit the road.

Harold: Oh hush up, would ya? Ya comin' ta dinner tonight at mama's and you can sleep in da guest room at my house and leave in da mornin'. It ain't no streetlights on them roads and I can tell you scared. Young Black man that don't know where he going, and it's dark too? Take the guest room.

Johnathan: That's a generous offer but-

Harold: No but's Sir Johnathan, I insist. Now come on and help me finish cleanin' up so we can get outta hea.

Johnathan: Help you clean? But I don't work here?

Harold: Ya hired boy! Grab that broom and let's get to it.

(Johnathan shakes his head and grabs the broom.)

CURTAIN.

ACT THREE

SCENE ONE

A table and chairs dressed for dinner sits in the middle of Junie Mae's dining room.

Lisa and Junie Mae are preparing the table for company.

Lisa: Mama I told you I was gonna make dinner tonight. I just don't understand how I get here and everything is almost ready.

Junie Mae: If I ain't start cooking when I did da meatloaf wasn't gon be ready by da time dinna supposed to start.

Lisa: I got here when I said I would, maybe a few minutes later.

Junie Mae: Dem few minutes make da difference between a hungry family and a full family. Plus Harold said you was tryna make something different tuhnight so I made da meatloaf for me. Just in case.

Lisa: Just in case you didn't like what I made?

Junie Mae: No just in case you lost yo mind and tried ta feed me something other den meatloaf and potatoes tuhnight. I been having meatloaf since I was young and ya thank ya was gon' serve something else up in dis house on dis day? Not up in here ya ain't.

Lisa: Mama we all know how important your meatloaf and potatoes is. It was just a quick thought that popped in and out of my head.

Junie Mae: If it was a quick thought den how Harold know bout it? He reading minds now?

Lisa: So maybe it wasn't a quick thought. But mama, we been eating meatloaf every last Friday night for as long as I can remember.

Junie Mae: And what's wrong with dat?

Lisa: Nothing wrong with it really, I just thought we could do something different tonight.

Junie Mae: What? Like habanatchi?

Lisa: What was that mama?

Junie Mae: You heard me. Hachabi. Whatever Harold said you was tryna make.

Lisa: Hibachi?

Junie Mae: You knew what I meant when I said what I said.

Lisa: Oh. Well I thought about it and decided against it. Too much salt... and I didn't want to break your tradition mama.

Junie Mae: And it's gon' stay dat way too. Don't be tryna change thangs Lisa. If it ain't broke don't fix it. Ain't dat what I tell you?

Lisa: Yes ma'am. But can I ask you something mama? I mean I know I can but sometimes you don't like us asking you things and I just want to know-

Junie Mae *(interrupting)*: Spit it out child!

Lisa: What's with the meatloaf and potatoes mama? Trust me, I love the meal but there has to be a reason you're so adamant about this meal.

Junie Mae: Dere is.

Lisa: How come you never told us why it's so special?

Junie Mae: How come you ain't never ask?

Lisa: I don't mean to be rude mama, but you aren't really the easiest person to talk to sometimes.

Junie Mae: What ya mean by dat? Ya can't talk ta me? Why ya think ya can't talk ta me?

Lisa: You're scary mama.

Junie Mae: Oh you just soft. You and your brother.

Lisa: Okay mama.

Junie Mae: If ya got something to ask, ask.

Lisa: I already did.

Junie Mae: What was it?

Lisa: Mama I asked why the meatloaf and potatoes was so special.

Junie Mae: Oh yeah.

(Junie Mae sits down.)

Junie Mae: Sit down, let me tell you.

(Lisa sits down.)

Junie Mae: When I was a little girl my family used ta have these same monthly meals. All da Warner's near and far would come in town and my grandmama and granddaddy would have these big feasts. Everybody would just come togetha and eat. I mean everything ya can think of would be on da table.

Lisa: I'm guessing there was meatloaf on the table too?

Junie Mae: Ya wanna tell it or ya want me to finish?

(Lisa zips her lips shut.)

Junie Mae: When I got old enough ta help cook, my grandma let me make da meatloaf and potatoes. She said it was easy enough. "It's just a loaf of meat and some taters" So every month family would come in town and eat da food dat me, my grandma and my grandpa made, including my daddy's brother, my uncle Johnnie B. He was my favorite family member. And trust me, there was a lot of family ta choose from. Johnnie B would come in town from wherever he was working and made sure he brought me something special from wherever he had come from. I got a whole collection of stuff he used ta give me. Kept it all ova da years too. He was a migrant worker so he went wherever da money was. But he always made sure ta come in town for my grandma and grandpa's feast at da end of da month. One of da last times I seen him is when he came in town and he told my daddy dat he was leaving to go up north. They argued about it because daddy told him there wasn't nothing for him up north and he would be safer closer ta family. But Johnnie B had his mind made up. Of course I was sad but all I could think about is him not showing up ta the feasts anymore. He always had said the meatloaf and potatoes was his favorite and he said he was going ta miss me and it da most. He had said he would be back to visit and I wanted ta make sure dat it was always dere whenever he made it back home. He never did. Dat was the last time I saw him.

Lisa: Mama, you never told us about any of this.

Junie Mae: Y'all ain't never think to ask me bout my life, I ain't never had no reason to talk about it.

Lisa: Mama, I never knew about a feast or a Johnnie B or none of this. I see why this is so important to you.

Junie Mae: Yeah, Johnnie B was my daddy's little brother. He hopped on the first thing smoking out of here the first chance he got, but like I said he always came back. Except when he didn't. Right when people kept migrating up north he kept saying that was going to be him one day. And one day it was. He packed up everything he had, which wasn't much, and moved up north. Daddy told me he heard Johnnie B made it up north somewhere. Dey hadn't talked since he left either. Stubborn old men, da both of dem.

Lisa: I see where you, I mean Harold, get it from.

Junie Mae: Be quiet, let me finish. What was I saying?

Lisa: You were telling me the story about your uncle Johnnie B and the meatloaf.

Junie Mae: Oh yeah. Johnnie B loved his meatloaf and potatoes. Even after he left and didn't come back I kept making it for da family feast and den when the feasts stopped I just decided ta keep making the meatloaf and potatoes fa myself and den fa y'all growing up.

Lisa: Mama I had no idea.

Junie Mae: Well now you do. Let me go check on my meatloaf. Da potatoes done already. Finish setting dis table. Harold and Missy should be here soon.

Lisa: Probably not together the way they went at it earlier. And mama you know she don't like being called Missy.

Junie Mae: I know da girl name Melissa.

(A doorbell rings.)

Lisa: That's probably one of them now. *(yelling)* Come on in!

(Melissa enters stage left.)

Melissa: Hey Auntie Lisa, hey grandma.

Lisa: Hey Melissa.

(Lisa stands up and gives her a hug.)

Junie Mae: Hey Mi... lissa. Come help me with dis food in da kitchen. Lisa finish setting the table up.

Melissa *(sarcastically)*: Straight to work. Yes. I love it here.

Junie Mae: What ya say gal?

Melissa: I said straight to work! Yes! I love it here!

(Junie Mae shakes her head and walks towards stage right.)

Melissa: Following you to the kitchen.

(Junie Mae and Melissa exit stage right. Lisa continues to set the table and hums a familiar tune. Beat. The doorbell rings.)

Lisa *(yelling)*: Come on in!

(Harold enters stage left.)

Harold: I know dat smell anywhere. Mama's meatloaf!

Lisa: Well how you know I didn't cook it?

Harold: Because yo meatloaf don't smell like mama meatloaf.

Lisa: You don't like my meatloaf?

Harold: Now I ain't say all that. Yo meatloaf good too. Mama's meatloaf just smells different. Ya can smell da love. Yerrs smells like you only make it because she tell ya to. No love smells.

Lisa: My meatloaf is made with love too.

Harold: Ain't no love in ya loaf. Just meat. It still taste good doe.

Lisa: Whatever, Harold. And thanks for tellin' mama about the hibachi by the way.

Harold: Ya welcome!

Lisa: Mama told me the reason she been making meatloaf this whole time. It's because of an old uncle of hers.

Harold: What? He used to make it fa her or somethin'?

Lisa: You want to tell it or you want me to finish?

Harold: Gon' head now. Soundin' like mama.

Lisa: Well apparently mama's family used to have these big monthly feasts when she was growing up. And when she got old enough they started to let her make the meatloaf.

Harold: And she still making it. Dat's a lot of meatloaf.

Lisa: Harold let me finish, will ya!?

Harold: Come on den, ya takin' so long!

Lisa: Anyway, she had this uncle that left town and never came back and she kept making it thinking he would and she just never stopped making it.

(Beat.)

Harold: Oh dat's the end?

Lisa: Yeah that's the end.

Harold: Well den... da meatloaf ready yet?

Lisa: I just told you that mama shared an intimate memory with me and that's all you got to say is "well then"?

Harold: What I'm posed ta say?

Lisa: Something a little more caring maybe?

Harold: Caring fa what? He gotta be long dead. Mama old and that was her uncle so unless he in the Ginny records, he dead dead.

Lisa: Caring for mama you old fool.

Harold: Aw mama don't care bout none of dat no mo'. Dat man long gone. I'm surprised she even remembered dat much.

Lisa: I don't know Harold. She seemed like it was just yesterday that all this was happening. Her uncle Johnnie B must've really meant something to her.

Harold: Johnnie B? Now why dat sound familiar?

(The doorbell rings.)

Harold *(yelling)*: Come on in!

Lisa: Harold who is that at the door you telling to come on in?

(Johnathan enters stage left.)

Harold: Sir Johnathan, glad to see ya made it in the house.

Johnathan: Sorry Mr. Harold, I had to make a quick phone call.

(Johnathan notices the smell.)

59

Johnathan: Wow that meatloaf smells good.

Harold: Yeah it do, don't it?

Johnathan: Just how my daddy house used to smell. Ms. Lisa you sure you don't know my family?

Lisa: Oh honey, I'm flattered but mama's actually the one that made it this time. Her and Melissa should be bringing in the main course any minute now from the kitchen.

Harold: Oh Lord, Missy here?

Lisa *(sternly)*: Call the girl by her name or don't call her at all. Not here and not tonight. You hear me Harold?

Harold: Yes ma'am mama Junie Mae junior.

(Melissa enters stage right and walks to the table carrying a pan of potatoes.)

Melissa: Oh hey! I guess you changed your mind about my aunt's invite.

Harold: Actually he didn't. I'm da one dat got him ta come ta mama house tuhnight.

(Johnathan walks around admiring the room to avoid conversation. Melissa ignores Harold.)

Harold: Uh hello ya don't hear me gal?

Melissa: I hear you talking dad.

Harold: Den ya need ta speak when ya spoken ta.

Melissa: I'm speaking to you now.

Harold: Don't sass me gal. We in my mama house and I ain't tryna start no mess witcha Missy.

(Melissa drops the pan onto the table. Jonathan walks intentionally the room again to be nosy.)

Melissa: I'm not doing this with you tonight.

Lisa: Nobody is doing anything tonight. We are going to sit and we are going to have dinner like a family. Is that clear? Y'all will not ruin this meal for my mama.

Harold: She my mama too!

Lisa: Is that clear?

Harold: Yea I hear ya.

Melissa: Yes ma'am.

(Harold starts to pick at the potatoes on the table. Beat.)

Melissa: Dad, there's actually something I need to talk to you about. I'm glad you're here too Auntie Lisa.

Harold: Whatchu want now Missy? I mean... (mockingly) Melissa?

Lisa: Harold.

Melissa: It's fine. I just wanted to let y'all know that I've decided to leave town. For good this time.

Lisa: Well I can't say I didn't see this coming. You sure about this? What am I saying? Of course you are. I'm sure you've thought long and hard about this decision.

Harold: She been miserable since she came back, I'm surprised it took this long.

(Johnathan stops walking.)

Johnathan: Not to be all up in y'all business again, Mr. Harold but-

Harold: Then don't be! If the gal wanna go, let 'er go!

Johnathan: Alright then.

(Johnathan starts walking again, fake admiring the room.)

Melissa: You don't even want me here.

Harold: Now why ya don't think I want ya here?

(Everybody looks at Harold.)

Harold: Aight, I get it. I just be talkin' sometimes. Don't mean I don't want ya round. But ain't nothin' fa ya hea so gon' on.

Melissa: You're not mad?

Harold: What I'm gon' be mad fa? I'm ya daddy and I'm supposed to take care of ya like my daddy did me and Lisa and his daddy did his kids too. We family. We take care of each other. Me takin' care of ya right now is me tellin' ya that ya should leave.

Melissa: Is that your idea of an apology?

Harold: What I'm apologizin' fa?

Lisa: Harold why can't you just apologize and tell the girl how you really feel.

(Johnathan stops walking again.)

Johnathan: What she said.

(Johnathan continues walking.)

Harold: What y'all want me to say that fa? And what ya walkin' around like dat fa boy? Ya makin' me nervous.

Johnathan: You know, I really don't know. It just has a real homely vibe to it. Like I been here before.

(Harold stares at Johnathan. Johnathan stops walking and sits down.)

Melissa: It's okay Auntie Lisa y'all. My mind is made up and my daddy knows how I feel now so I'm good.

Harold: Good fa ya making ya mind up. Now when can we eat?

Melissa: You'll be proud of me one day dad.

Harold: Now I ain't never said I ain't proud of ya Melissa. I don't agree with a lot of what ya do but that ain't never meant I ain't proud of ya. Even doe ya hate me, for whatever reason, I always want ya ta be happy and if ya need ta leave ta do dat den do it.

Because clearly ya ain't happy hea. I done seen ya bags packed in ya room since last week and I came to terms witcha leavin' already.

(Melissa hugs Harold.)

Melissa: I don't hate you dad.

Harold: Yea, alright Melissa. Why we ain't eatin' yet?

Melissa: We can finish this conversation later I guess. Grandma!

(Melissa heads towards stage right to exit as Junie Mae is entering.)

Junie Mae: Oh you gon' ahead and turn around Melissa. This the third time you bumpin' in ta me today. Whatever ya daddy said he ain't meant it.

Melissa: Oh no grandma, it's not like that... this time.

(Junie Mae grabs Melissa's hand and walks her back to the table. She notices Johnathan and stops dead in her tracks.)

Junie Mae: Johnnie B.

Johnathan: Ma'am?

(Junie Mae is still staring at Johnathan, speechless and in shock. Beat.)

Johnathan: I'm sorry, but this is getting weird.

Junie Mae: I never thought I'd see that face again.

Johnathan: My face?

Lisa: Mama what you talking about? You feeling okay?

(Junie Mae snaps out of her trance. She walks up to Johnathan to admire him up close. She gets excited.)

Harold: Mama why ya touchin' on da boy like that? Ain't you too old ta not know bout stranga danga?

Junie Mae: Shut up Harold. This boy ain't no stranger, he's family.

Johnathan: Excuse me, what's going on?

Melissa: Yeah grandma, what's going on?

Junie Mae: What's your name young man?

Johnathan: Johnathan Barnes the Third ma'am.

Junie Mae: Ha! Johnathan Barnes. Ain't nobody named Johnathan Barnes. You Johnnie B Warner the Third. Wow you look just like him. I couldn't forget dat old mug if I tried.

(Junie Mae touches his face and turns his head side to side.)

Harold: Mama stop touchin' on da boy face! Now come on now, we tryna figure out whatcha talkin' about.

Johnathan: Wait, you knew my grandfather?

(Johnathan stands up and shows Junie Mae the picture from his pocket. Her excitement fades and she exits stage right.)

Harold: What is goin' on!?

(Junie Mae enters stage right with a photo album. She turns to a specific page and points.)

Johnathan: My grandfather.

Junie Mae: And my father Henry. His older brother.

(Johnathan is speechless.)

Junie Mae: Johnnie B Warner the Third.

(Johnathan sits down to take in all the information he received.)

Harold: Excuse me ma'ma, Sir Johnnie B Warner da Third, I don't mean ta interrupt but da food getting cold.

Junie Mae: Hush up Harold! Gon' head and eat if ya that hungry. And I hope ya got some gas pills too. Ya know how ya get.

Harold: Don't worry bout dat mama, I got some from Lisa earlier tuhday!

(Harold sits down and grabs a plate of food. He bows his head quickly.)

Harold: Amen.

(Harold eats his food as if he hadn't eaten all day.)

Johnathan: Can you tell me about him?

Junie Mae: Well that all depends on how much time you got.

Harold *(in between bites of food)*: He got time mama. He stayin' at my house in the guess room fa da night.

Johnathan: I'll be here as long as I need to be. Please just tell me everything you can remember about my grandfather.

Junie Mae: The memories I have of your grandfather could never fade away, no matter how old I may get. I'll tell you everything that you want to know and den some young man.

CURTAIN.

END OF PLAY.